EXPLORING SCIENCE

SOIL

DIGGING INTO EARTH'S VITAL RESOURCE

BY DARLENE R. STILLE

Content Adviser: Jim Walker, Professor of Geology and
Environmental Geosciences, Northern Illinois University

Science Adviser: Terrence E. Young Jr., M.Ed., M.L.S.,
Jefferson Parish (Louisiana) Public School System

Reading Adviser: Susan Kesselring, M.A., Literacy Educator,
Rosemount-Apple Valley-Eagan (Minnesota) School District

 COMPASS POINT BOOKS · MINNEAPOLIS, MINNESOTA

Compass Point Books • 3109 West 50th Street, #115 • Minneapolis, MN 55410

Visit Compass Point Books on the Internet at *www.compasspointbooks.com*
or e-mail your request to *custserv@compasspointbooks.com*

Photographs ©: Joseph Sohm; ChromoSohm Inc./Corbis, cover; Charles O'Rear/Corbis, 4; Scott T. Smith/Corbis, 5, 32; D. Robert & Lorri Franz/Corbis, 6; Seattle Art Museum/Corbis, 7; USDA/ARS, 9; Wally Eberhart/Visuals Unlimited, 10; Richard Hamilton Smith, 13, 36; Matt Meadows/Peter Arnold, Inc., 14; Deborah Kopp/Visuals Unlimited, 15; Tommy Dodson/Unicorn Stock Photos, 16; Phil Schermeister/Peter Arnold, Inc., 17; Macduff Everton/Corbis, 18–19, 43; Marli Miller/Visuals Unlimited, 20; Kevin Fleming/Corbis, 22–23; Lynn Rogers/Peter Arnold, Inc., 24; Larry Stepanowicz/Visuals Unlimited, 25; Natalie Fobes/Corbis, 27; Raymond C. Murray, author of Evidence from the Earth - Forensic Geology and Criminal Investigation, Mountain Press 2004, 29; University of Idaho, 30 ; University of Idaho/Dr. Paul McDaniel, 31 (left); Reproduced from Soils of the Great Plains: Land Use, Crops and Grasses by permission of the University of Nebraska Press, 31 (right); Eric LeNorcy/Peter Arnold, Inc., 34; Alex S. MacLean/Peter Arnold, 35; David Turnley/Corbis, 37; Fred Bruemmer/Peter Arnold, Inc., 38; Richard Hamilton Smith/Corbis, 39; Joe Sohm; ChromoSohm Inc./Unicorn Stock Photos, 40; Steve Strickland/Corbis, 44; Luiz C. Marigo/Peter Arnold Inc., 46.

Art Director: Keith Griffin
Managing Editor: Catherine Neitge
Editor: Nadia Higgins
Photo Researcher: Marcie C. Spence
Designer/Page production: The Design Lab
Lead Designer: Jaime Martins
Illustrator: Farhana Hossain
Educational Consultant: Diane Smolinski

Library of Congress Cataloging-in-Publication Data
Stille, Darlene R.
    Soil : digging into Earth's vital resource / by Darlene R. Stille.
        p. cm. — (Exploring science)
    Includes bibliographical references and index.
    ISBN 0-7565-0857-6 (hardcover)
    1. Soils—Juvenile literature. I. Title. II. Exploring science (Minneapolis, Minn.)
    S591.3.S745 2005
    631.4—dc22   2004019872

About the Author

Darlene R. Stille is a science writer and author of more than 70 books for young people. When she was in high school, she fell in love with science. While attending the University of Illinois, she discovered that she also loved writing. She was fortunate enough to find a career as an editor and writer that allowed her to combine both of her interests. Darlene Stille now lives and writes in Michigan.

TABLE OF CONTENTS

CHAPTER ONE

Soil: It's Not Plain Dirt

YOU WALK ALL OVER IT. You get it on your shoes. If you track it into the house, you might think of it as dirt. It's soil, and there is a lot more to soil than just plain dirt.

Soil covers most of Earth's land. It can be just a few inches or several feet thick. Soil makes up soft forest floors, green front yards, and sandy beaches. It is dry desert sand and rich farmland, sticky riverbanks and soggy marshes.

Different plants thrive in different types of soil. Dark, rich soil is best for growing grapevines at a vineyard.

There could be no life on Earth without soil. Virtually all food comes directly or indirectly from soil. The food chain begins with plants that grow in soil. We eat these plants and also the meat from plant-eating animals and the eggs and dairy products they provide. There is practically not a single food in the grocery store that does not depend on soil.

That is just the beginning of the soil story. The oxygen that you breathe comes from plants that grow in soil. Plants take in carbon dioxide gas from the air. When plants respire, or "breathe out," they give off oxygen, a gas that all animals need for life.

A yucca plant can grow in dry, sandy soil.

A wide variety of animals call soil their home. The soil is alive with microscopic creatures such as bacteria and fungi. Worms tunnel around in the soil. Mammals dig burrows. Soil provides underground homes for rabbits, moles, snakes, gophers, and groundhogs.

Soil has uses in industry, too. Bricks are made directly from soil, while wood for lumber comes from trees that grow in it. Cloths such as linen and cotton come from plants that rely on soil, as do many types of dyes and medicines.

A black-footed ferret peeks out of its burrow. It is one of billions of creatures that live in soil.

African Mud Cloth

Some soils can be used to create works of art. Potters use clay, for example, to mold beautiful plates, cups, vases, and jars.

People who live in the African nation of Mali use mud to create a unique kind of cloth called *bogolanfini,* or "mud cloth." Women are the main creators of this mud cloth, and mothers pass the secrets of their technique along to their daughters.

text continued on page 8

An example of *bogolanfini* (African mud cloth) from the Seattle Art Museum in Washington

continued from page 7

The process begins with plain white cotton, which is washed so that it may shrink. The women then coat the cloth with a liquid solution made from leaves. When the cloth dries, it turns yellow.

Next, the women paint the cloth using a black solution made from rich mud. The mud was collected from ponds and kept in a pot for about a year. With the mud, the women draw around the yellow areas to create a design.

Finally, the women apply another solution that causes chemical reactions in the cloth. This last step turns the yellow areas white again and makes the black areas colorfast. The finished cloth has stark white lines that make patterns against a black background.

But the story of soil does not always have a happy ending. As the world's population grows, Earth is getting crowded with people to feed. Farmers want to use as much of the land as possible. However, overuse and mismanagement of land is damaging Earth's soil at astonishing rates.

Farmers, scientists, and government leaders are working to address this problem. Soil scientists, called pedologists, study what soil is made of and where it comes from. They monitor dangers to soil and try to figure out how best to protect it. Agricul-

tural scientists, called agronomists, have been working on finding ways to make the soil produce more food.

What does all this have to do with you? Choices you make
at the grocery store or garden center can have an impact on
soil. Should you buy organic produce? Should you put chemical fertilizer on your garden, or is there a better way to improve
the soil? Understanding the importance of soil and the things
that can harm it is the first step toward preserving this vital
natural resource.

An agronomist (far left) and other researchers with the U.S. Department
of Agriculture (USDA) remove pieces of a plant for study.

CHAPTER TWO

What Are the Components of Soil?

SOIL IS A MIXTURE of air, water, mineral particles, and decayed (or rotted) plants and animals. Scientists call the mineral particles inorganic material. The particles made up of dead plants and animals are called organic material.

The three types of inorganic particles are sand, silt, and clay. The difference between these particles is size. Sand is the largest kind of

From left: sand, silt, and clay

inorganic particle found in soil. You can scoop up a handful of sand from a beach and easily see a single grain of sand. Silt particles are smaller than sand. Clay particles are the smallest of all. You can only see a clay particle under a microscope.

Air and water fill the spaces between the organic and inorganic particles. Plant roots grow down into these spaces. The roots absorb water and nutrients from the soil. Nutrients are nourishing chemicals essential for life and health.

WHERE DO THE MINERAL PARTICLES COME FROM?

The mineral particles, or inorganic materials, in soil come from solid rock that is broken apart by natural processes called weathering. There are two kinds of weathering—physical weathering and chemical weathering. Physical weathering breaks the rocks into small pieces, but the chemical makeup of the material is not

FAST FACT: Good soil needs the right mix of air and water in its spaces. Half air and half water is the best mix for growing plants. Soils that have more air than water tend to be dry, like the soil of deserts. If the spaces between particles have more water than air, the soil is soggy, like the soils of bogs and marshes. Trees and other woody plants cannot grow in the soggy soil.

changed. Chemical weathering breaks down the rocks by changing minerals in the rocks to new minerals and other substances.

Sand and silt are formed by physical weathering. In physical weathering, rain, snow, sleet, and hail pound away at rocks to wear them down. Wind blasts away at the rocky surface, tearing off small pieces. Plant roots twist and turn in the tiny cracks of a rock. Though roots seem slender and fragile, they have the power to split a rock apart.

Most physical weathering, however, is caused by freezing and thawing. Water seeps into tiny cracks in the rock. The weather turns cold, and the water freezes. When water changes into ice, it expands. The force of the expanding ice is great enough to crack the rock.

Clay minerals are one of the important products of chemical weathering. This process is caused mainly by the chemicals in water. As water flows or drips over rocks, it slowly eats away at the rock. The chemicals in the water combine with minerals in the rock to make new substances.

Both physical and chemical weathering are gradual processes that take thousands of years. Weathering first breaks huge slabs of rock into boulders and stones. Further weathering breaks the boulders and stones into pebbles and gravel. Then, the pebbles and gravel get broken down into tiny particles of sand, silt, or clay.

Opposite page: An icicle inside a rock can crack the rock, leading to further weathering.

WHERE DO THE ORGANIC PARTICLES COME FROM?

The organic particles in soil come from dead plants and animals. They can also come from animal waste, which is called manure. Microscopic creatures that live in dirt, such as bacteria and fungi, are what cause the organic matter to decay. These tiny creatures are called decomposers. They break down plants and the bodies of insects and larger animals.

The organic particles form humus, a soft, spongy substance. Humus is black or dark brown and is found most often in the top layer of soil. Soils that have lots of humus are fertile, which means they are good for growing plants. They hold water and are rich with nutrients.

FAST FACT: One handful of soil holds billions of microscopic living creatures.

Plants and animals decay to form humus, the organic material in soil that makes it fertile.

CHAPTER THREE

How Does Soil Form?

AT LEAST FIVE conditions work together to form soil. Scientists call these the factors of soil formation. They are parent material, topography, organisms, climate, and time.

PARENT MATERIAL

The first factor is the parent material, which is the original material from which the soil formed. Often it's a layer of solid rock, or bedrock, that lies underneath the soil. The soil has the same kinds of minerals as the bedrock, or parent material, did. In this case, weathering broke the bedrock down into mineral particles, which stayed on top of the rock.

The parent material could have come from a faraway rock as well. After weathering broke up the rock, the mineral particles were moved by any number of methods. Water in a rushing river or a creeping glacier could have moved the particles. Or perhaps they were swept up by the wind and blown to a distant prairie.

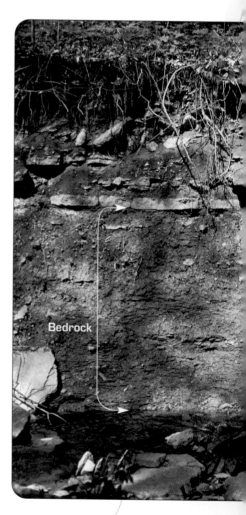

Bedrock

Bedrock supports the soil above it. When bedrock breaks down, it often becomes the parent material for the soil above it.

The parent material could have slid miles down the side of a hill or mountain, landing where it is today.

TOPOGRAPHY

The second factor is topography, which refers to kinds of landscapes, such as hills, mountains, and valleys. Soil layers on a hillside are thinner and drier than soils at the bottom of a hill. That's because water runs down the slope of a hill. As it flows downhill, water also erodes, or carries away, soil on the hillside and dumps it at the base of the hill.

On tall, steep mountains, soil is constantly being washed downhill—so much so that sometimes the entire layer of soil erodes, exposing the bedrock underneath. The forces of weathering then go to work, breaking the bedrock into mineral particles, which will someday form new soil.

A waterfall has eroded a mountainside, exposing the bedrock beneath the soil.

ORGANISMS—PLANTS AND ANIMALS

Plants and animals make soil that is good for growing. When plants die, they decay and become humus. This makes a patch of soil rich and fertile so even more plants and animals can thrive there.

Plants attract hungry animals, which also help the soil. As they wriggle, worms and other animals churn up the soil. They make spaces called pores between the soil particles. The pores fill with air or water, which allows plant roots to grow more easily. When the animals die, they also decay and become humus.

Plant roots make channels in the soil that cause pores, which in turn allows more air and water in. Like long, thin fingers, the roots of plants also help hold soil in place. The longer the soil stays in place, the better. As it sits, soil grows rich and deep. It collects more mineral particles from weathering rocks and humus from decaying plants and animals.

Tree roots prevent erosion by holding soil in place.

CLIMATE

How quickly soil forms depends on climate. Soil forms most quickly in places with warm, wet climates. Since chemical weathering relies on water, it is the main form of weathering in these climates. This chemical weathering causes a lot of clay in the soil. Also, dead plants and animals decay faster in warm, wet conditions, so soils that develop in these climates are rich in organic particles.

Soil forms more slowly in places with dry climates. With little water for chemical weathering, rocks in these places are usually broken up by physical weathering alone. The microscopic creatures that cause decay don't thrive in these climates either, so humus develops slowly. These soils contain more

Because it formed in a dry climate, desert soil is sandy and does not have a lot of humus.

mineral particles than organic particles and are not as fertile.

In temperate climates, soils form during the warm springs and summers. In winter and fall, cold temperatures slow down soil formation.

TIME

All these factors work together over time. Unless it is easily eroded, soil that sits over a long period of time becomes deep and rich.

Soils are constantly changing, but soils that stay in one place have many thick layers called horizons. It can take thousands of years for layers, or horizons, of rich, deep soil to form.

CHAPTER FOUR

Soil Horizons and Their Properties

IF YOU CUT out a slice of soil as you would cut out a piece of cake, you would see layers. The layered slice is called the soil profile. The main horizons in a slice of soil are called the A, B, and C horizons.

In some soil profiles, you can see sharp differences between each horizon, like the difference between layers of yellow and chocolate cake. In other soil profiles, the horizons seem to blend together. In addition, the horizons in one soil profile may be thick and in another, thin.

A soil profile showing soil horizons

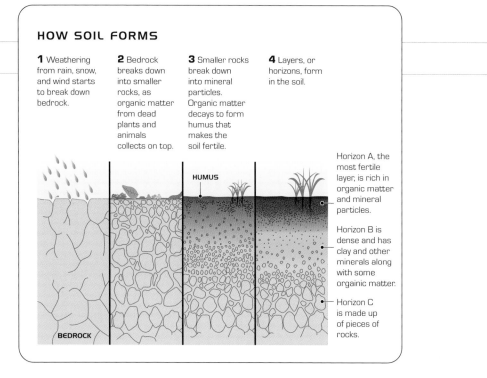

HOW SOIL FORMS

1 Weathering from rain, snow, and wind starts to break down bedrock.

2 Bedrock breaks down into smaller rocks, as organic matter from dead plants and animals collects on top.

3 Smaller rocks break down into mineral particles. Organic matter decays to form humus that makes the soil fertile.

4 Layers, or horizons, form in the soil.

HUMUS

BEDROCK

Horizon A, the most fertile layer, is rich in organic matter and mineral particles.

Horizon B is dense and has clay and other minerals along with some orgainic matter.

Horizon C is made up of pieces of rocks.

WHAT ARE THE HORIZONS MADE OF?

The A horizon is the top layer of soil. This horizon is also called topsoil. The A horizon is the most fertile because it contains the most air, water, and humus.

Leaves and other parts that fall off of plants are called litter. Litter lands on the A horizon, eventually decaying and turning into humus. Litter also keeps water from evaporating out of the soil and helps prevent erosion.

The B horizon is just below the A horizon. There is less humus in the B horizon, but nutrients from the A horizon drip down to the B horizon. This process is called leaching. Deep-rooting plants grow down through the A horizon and take up the nutrients in the B horizon.

The C horizon is below the B horizon and on top of the underlying bedrock. The C horizon is called subsoil. The C horizon is the least weathered layer. It is made up almost entirely of pieces of rock that are like the bedrock below it.

Pedologists study the properties of the soil in each horizon. They use the properties to describe the soil.

WHAT ARE SOIL PROPERTIES?

The way the five soil-forming factors interact is always different from one place to another, so soils differ greatly from each other. Each section of soil on a landscape has its own characteristics, or properties. Color, texture, structure, and chemical makeup are some of the properties that scientists use to describe soil.

Soil comes in many colors—from yellow to red to gray, brown, or black. Color tells scientists what is in the soil. Red soils, for example, contain lots of the chemical element iron. Dark brown or black soils are rich in humus. The darker a soil, the more organic material it contains.

Red soil on a farm in Georgia is a sign that the land contains a lot of iron.

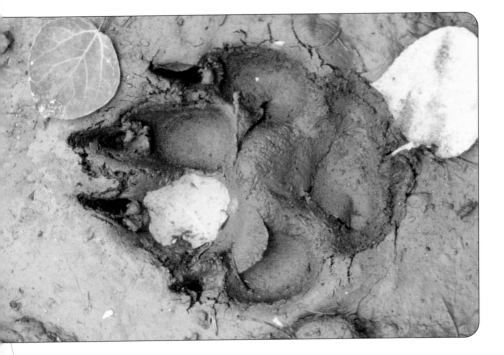

The texture of a soil comes from the inorganic particles. Most soils are a mixture of sand, silt, and clay. The amount of sand, silt, or clay in soil determines its texture. Soils with a lot of sand are coarse and loose. They have good drainage, which means water flows easily through them. Silty soils are smooth and powdery.

Soils with a lot of clay are smooth and sticky. The sticky soil holds nutrients needed for plant growth. Too much clay, however, can hurt plants. Because the particles are so tiny, they pack firmly and can keep air and water out of the soil.

Wet, sticky soil with a lot of clay holds the mold of a wolf track well.

Soil pH

How can scientists know if a soil is acidic or alkaline or neutral?
They use a measurement called the pH scale.

Numbers on the pH scale go from 0 to 14, with pH 7 as the
neutral point. A solution having a pH from 0 to 7 is an acid.
Lemon juice, for example, is very acidic. A solution having a pH
between 7 and 14 is an
alkali, or base. Household
drain cleaners are very
alkaline. Pure water has a
pH of 7.

To measure pH, a soil
scientist first mixes some
soil with pure water to
make a solution. The most
accurate way to find a soil
pH is by using an electronic
pH meter. A cheaper, but
less accurate, method uses
special strips of test paper.
The strips change color
depending on how acidic or
alkaline the soil solution is.

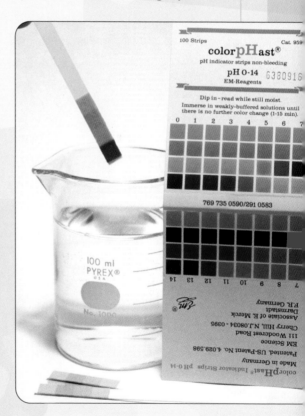

text continued on page 26

One way to test a solution's acidity is to dip pH paper strips in it. The paper changes color. Each color
represents a range on the pH scale. Strips of pH paper vary greatly in their degree of precision.

continued from page 25

Different plants grow best in soils with different pH numbers. For example, soils with a pH between 5.5 and 7 are best for growing alfalfa. Bacteria that live in alfalfa plants convert nitrogen in air to a form the plants can use. The bacteria thrive when the soil pH is above 5.5. Soils with a pH between 6 and 7 are best for soybeans. Those with a pH between 5.3 and 6.6 are great for growing peanuts.

Chemical pest killers will not work in soils that are too acidic. When it rains, the chemicals will just run off and pollute nearby lakes, streams, or groundwater.

Soil structure comes from the way soil particles aggregate, or stick together, even through cycles of wetting and drying. Sand, silt, and clay form clumps called peds, which can be shaped like thin plates, columns, or blocks. They can be so tiny that they are microscopic, or they can be the size of large boulders.

The chemistry of a soil can make it acidic, alkaline (the opposite of acidic), or neutral (neither acidic nor alkaline). Most plants grow best in neutral soils. Plants also need certain chemical elements to grow and be healthy. Among the most important elements are nitrogen, phosphorus, and potassium. Each element helps create healthy plant parts. Nitrogen is good for leaves and stems; phosphorus, for roots; and potassium, for flowers.

WHY ARE SOIL PROPERTIES IMPORTANT?

When soil scientists know the properties of a soil profile, they can predict what plants will grow best in the soil and how the soil will behave during droughts and floods. For example, soil with a structure of small, block-shaped peds holds water well.

The chemistry of a soil can tell if the soil needs to have substances added in order to grow good crops. If the soil in a farm field lacks nitrogen, phosphorous, or potassium, the farmer could add these elements by applying chemical fertilizer.

Soil scientists also use soil properties to analyze and describe an area of soil. This helps them determine how many soil types there are.

A soil scientist in Knight Island, Alaska, lies down on the land to get a good smell. He is checking for oil content.

Solving Crimes with Soil

It was a dark night on the farm, when shadowy figures slipped into the barn and filled sack after sack with newly harvested potatoes. The farmer woke the next morning to discover he had been robbed. It seemed like the perfect crime. There was not a single clue.

Then, a few days later, a market owner called the police and reported that strangers were trying to sell him some potatoes. The police picked up the suspects. They thought they had the potato thieves, but they needed more proof.

Though this story is not real, what the police would do next is real. They might call a forensic geologist. In our story, her name is Molly Mudd.

Molly Mudd, like all forensic geologists, studies soil to help solve crimes. First, she went to the farm and took soil samples from the potato field. Then she took samples of soil from the potatoes the suspects were trying to sell.

Molly knew that soil differs from place to place. The soil profiles in the farmer's potato field would be different from those on any other farm, so Molly went to work. She examined particle sizes in the samples from the potatoes and from the field. She looked for telltale minerals with a special microscope. If the soil properties were different in the two samples, the police would have to let the suspects go. But the soils matched!

The case was solved, and the suspects were found guilty.

Forensic geologists are called in to help solve thousands of criminal cases in the United States each year, including serious crimes such as murder and robbery. Technicians collect soil samples from the crime scene and send them to a crime lab for study. The U.S. Federal Bureau of Investigation (FBI) started using forensic geology in 1935. It has become a common investigation tool today.

A soil collector (bottom left) takes samples from the scene of a hit-and-run car accident in Missoula, Montana.

CHAPTER FIVE

⊕ Soil Types

IT MIGHT SEEM at first that there would only be a few types of soil, such as sandy soil or soil with a lot of clay. But, according to the U.S. Department of Agriculture (USDA), there are more than 50,000 different soils in the United States alone. Soil type depends on how and when soil formed. Soil types vary from state to state, field to field, and even in places within the same field.

Soil scientists have a system for classifying soils just as biologists have systems for classifying animals and plants. The most general classification level is the soil order. There are 12 soil orders, followed by suborders, groups, and subgroups. The lowest classification level is the soil series. By classifying soils in this way, scientists keep track of thousands of soil types.

Spodosol

Aridisol

SOIL ORDERS

Name	Where it forms	Characteristics	% of Earth's soil by area
Alfisol	grasslands and forests, humid climates	good for agriculture	9.7
Andisol	areas with volcanic ash	holds a lot of water	0.7
Aridisol	dry regions, deserts	few organic particles	12.0
Entisol	all over and in all climates	strongly resembles parent material; includes all soils that don't fit in other orders	16.2
Gelisol	polar regions, high mountaintops	frozen	8.6
Histosol	wet places; swamps and bogs	lots of organic material	1.2
Inceptisol	more common in humid areas but found all over	resembles parent material; thin horizons	9.8
Mollisol	prairie regions	thick, rich topsoil; fertile	21.5
Oxisol	tropical regions	chemically weathered with reddish color; low nutrient levels	7.5
Spodosol	cool, humid regions such as pine forests	acidic	2.6
Ultisol	warm, humid regions	moist, acidic	8.5
Vertisol	relatively dry, warm regions	has a lot of clay; can develop deep, wide cracks when not much rain	2.4

Sources: USDA Natural Resources Conservation Service, World Book Multimedia Encyclopedia, University of Idaho's College of Agricultural and Life Sciences

Vertisol

Oxisol

MAKING SOIL MAPS

Just as physical maps show where mountains, lakes, and rivers are located, soil maps show where different soils are located. Soil maps can show orders, suborders, or more specific classifications of soil.

To begin making a map of soil orders, a soil scientist identifies areas with similar soil-forming factors, such as climate and parent material. Most areas in the Midwestern United States, for example, have a warm, humid climate. The parent material in

the Midwest is a kind of silt called loess, which blew in from the edges of ancient glaciers. Soil map makers usually find thick A horizons here, formed by prairie grasses that decayed and formed humus. In deserts, they find light-colored A horizons with very little humus. In forests, they find B horizons that contain a lot of clay.

A scientist collects data for making a soil map.

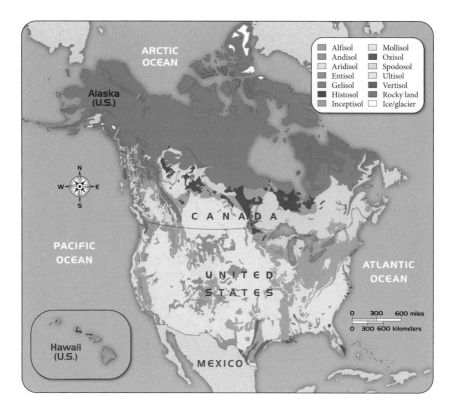

Making an atlas of soil maps is like making an atlas of other maps. First, soil scientists map the big picture—the location of soil orders across the country. This map is like a road map showing the interstate highway system across the United States.

Within a large region, such as the Midwest, they can make more detailed maps of smaller and smaller areas—from states to counties to individual townships. These maps for finding patches of soil are like city maps that help you find a particular street.

A map showing areas covered by the 12 main soil orders in the United States and Canada

Wise Use of Soil

ONE OF THE GREATEST problems in our world is the issue of vanishing farmland. Worldwide, soil suitable for farming is disappearing up to 40 times faster than nature can replace it. What is causing such fast rates of soil loss? And what can be done about it?

PREVENTING EROSION

Erosion causes much soil loss. Cutting down trees in forests and digging up grasses on prairies exposes the soil to the forces of

wind and rain, which will blow or wash soil away. Herds of cattle left to graze without proper management will eat every plant in sight, exposing rangeland to erosion.

There will always be some erosion, but farmers have learned ways to minimize it. Planting trees and shrubs between farm fields breaks the force of wind, reducing wind erosion of soil.

Building terraces on steep hills can help prevent water erosion. Terraces are flat steps built into the side of a hill. Farmers plant their crops on each flat terrace. The terraces

Terraces covered by rice plants in Bali, Indonesia, slow the flow of water down the hill, thereby preventing erosion.

keep water from rushing down the hill's slope and taking precious soil with it. Terraced fields are popular in the hills of India and Southeast Asia.

Certain methods of plowing or tilling fields can lessen both water and wind erosion. Tilling loosens the soil so that seeds can be buried. But the loosened soil is also more likely to dry out and blow away. Using a technique called contour plowing, farmers till across the slope of a hill, not up and down. This makes ridges in the soil that catch water and slow its flow downhill.

In highly eroded places, farmers do not till the soil at all. In no-till farming, the stalks of the last year's crops are left on the ground to provide a cover, or mulch, for the soil. Then the farmer sprays the field with an herbicide to kill weeds before planting new seed. The drawback to this method is that herbicides can cause water pollution.

Contour plowing on a hillside in Iowa

PREVENTING SOIL DAMAGE

Soil can also be seriously damaged by factors beside erosion. Planting crops over and over again on the same field can wear

out soil, leaving it poor in essential nutrients. Farmers have long looked for ways to prevent soil from wearing out. The ancient Romans divided a farm into two fields. They plowed both fields but planted a crop in only one. They left the other field to lie fallow, or unseeded, so it could recover nutrients.

Modern farmers want to use every inch of farmland to produce crops every year and feed an ever-growing population. So they replace lost nutrients with fertilizers. Most farm fertilizers are

On this no-till soybean field, last year's crops are left on the ground to preserve the soil.

chemicals, and they cause pollution in lakes and rivers when rainwater washes them out of the soil.

Too much chemical fertilizer can also kill some of the tiny creatures that help decay. By killing these decomposers, fertilizer can slow the development of humus in soil. Environmental scientists believe that using organic farming methods might solve these problems.

Farmers have learned how to make deserts bloom through irrigation, which is bringing water to the dry soil. However, when the irrigation water gets used by plants or evaporates, it leaves salts behind that can poison the soil. Farmers try to

A farmer sprinkles chemical fertilizer on his crops.

reduce this damage by using the best irrigation methods they can. They irrigate at night when temperatures are cooler so water will not evaporate as quickly. They also might choose crops that don't use a lot of water.

WHAT IS ORGANIC FARMING?

Organic farming replaces chemical fertilizers and pesticides with natural ways of fertilizing fields and eliminating pests. Organic farmers use fertilizers made from manure and other waste products. They create "green manure" by planting certain crops and then plowing them into the ground.

Rotating sprinkler systems create circular plots of irrigated land in the Mojave Desert, California.

They rotate crops by planting a different crop in every field each year. Alfalfa, clover, beans, or other legumes are good rotation crops, because legumes replace nitrogen in the soil that other plants take out. Legumes also make good green manure.

Rotating crops is also a method of pest control, because it disrupts the habitats of pests. Organic farmers encourage a rich diversity of beneficial insects and birds to help control pests.

Organic crops, however, are more expensive to produce and therefore cost more at the store. Also, an organic field yields from 5 to 20 percent less food than a conventional farm field.

FAST FACT: One natural way that gardeners can make their grass stronger is simply by watering it less often. This dries out the upper soil horizon, which causes roots to grow deeper in the soil in search of water.

A manure spreader at work on an organic farm

Make Your Own Compost

Compost is a rich organic fertilizer that gardeners can use to make grass, flowers, and vegetables grow better. Not only is compost a great substitute for chemical fertilizers, it also helps get rid of garbage that might otherwise go to a landfill. You make compost the same way that nature makes humus—by using decayed plant parts or other organic material.

If you have some space outdoors, you can make this organic

fertilizer in your own compost pile. First, find a container to hold your compost. You can buy a composting kit or make your own. You can make a bin out of wire mesh or use an old plastic garbage container with holes poked in the sides. Set your compost pile up in the back of your yard or garden. It will attract earthworms and other decomposers.

To start the decay process, the compost pile

Hay and kitchen scraps provide a good balance of brown and green material for a compost pile.

needs wastes that contain carbon (so-called brown material) and wastes that contain nitrogen (green material). Newspaper, coffee grounds, and dead leaves contain carbon. Grass clippings, weeds, and leftover dinner vegetables contain nitrogen. Never put meat or dairy products in a compost pile since they attract animals that might dig up the pile. Add alternating layers of brown and green material. Throw in some soil between the layers. Keep adding to the pile until it is at least 3 feet (2.73 meters) tall.

Using a garden shovel, turn and mix your compost pile about once a week. This is to make sure the compost gets oxygen, which is necessary for the tiny creatures that are breaking down the material. Also, decay generates heat. The center of your pile could get up to 120 degrees Fahrenheit (49 degrees Celsius). When you turn the pile, you quicken the process by exposing all the material to this heat, which is another key factor in decomposition.

Every time you turn your pile, be sure to water it with a hose. That will speed up the process, too.

It could take anywhere from one month to seven months for compost to form. Compost is ready to use when it is a rich, dark brown. If you start a compost pile in the fall, by spring it may be ready to mix with the soil or spread on top as a mulch to hold moisture.

A COMPLEX PROBLEM

Solving the problem of our vanishing soil is not a simple task. The needs of people must be balanced against the needs of the entire planet.

The population of the world is skyrocketing. From just 1987 to 2000, it went up by 1 billion people—an increase of 20 percent. Government leaders fear there will not be enough food for everyone.

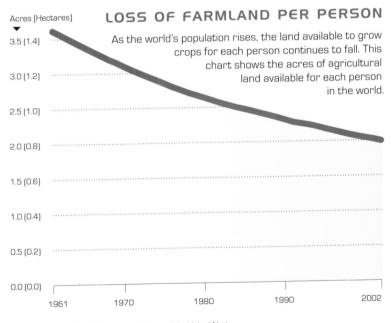

Acres (Hectares)

LOSS OF FARMLAND PER PERSON

As the world's population rises, the land available to grow crops for each person continues to fall. This chart shows the acres of agricultural land available for each person in the world.

3.5 (1.4)				
3.0 (1.2)				
2.5 (1.0)				
2.0 (0.8)				
1.5 (0.6)				
1.0 (0.4)				
0.5 (0.2)				
0.0 (0.0)				
1961	1970	1980	1990	2002

SOURCE: Food and Agricuture Organization of the United Nations

Scientists and policy makers are working hard to find a solution to this problem. Unfortunately, every answer seems to create a new problem. Chemical fertilizers and pesticides have greatly increased crop yields. But they have added to the pollution problem. Organic farming eliminates the pollution problem, but organic foods might be unaffordable for some people. In addition, organic crops don't make as much food as those produced with chemicals.

A farmer stands in front of a corn field on an organic farm. Organic farms make up less than 1 percent of all farms in the United States, according to the 2002 U.S. Census of Agriculture.

So far, no method found is perfect, but soil conservationists encourage growers to use an approach called wise use of soil. Wise use calls upon farmers to keep high levels of nutrients and organic matter in their soils. Farmers can add organic matter to the soil with green manure and by rotating crops. They can also add limited amounts of chemical fertilizer to provide adequate nutrients. They can control erosion with wise use of plowing and planting techniques.

One thing is clear, though. If the world continues to lose soil faster than it can be replaced, there will not be enough soil to raise sufficient food crops, no matter what farming method is used.

An airplane, called a crop duster, spreads pesticides on a field.

bacteria—single-celled microscopic creatures that exist everywhere in nature

carbon dioxide—a gas in the air that animals give off and plants use to make food

conservationist—someone who works to protect Earth's natural resources

fertile—good for growing crops

fertilizer—substances, such as manure or chemicals, to make soil richer and better for growing crops

fungi—mildews, molds, mushrooms, and other organisms that lack chlorophyll, the substance in plants that makes them green

glacier—huge mass of slow-moving ice

habitats—where plants or animals live in their natural states

herbicide—a chemical used to kill plants

inorganic—not from animals or plants

irrigation—bringing water to dry soil through methods such as pipes and channels

legumes—plants such as beans and peas that can convert nitrogen into a form other plants can use

minerals—solid materials that make up rocks

mulch—a protective covering of plants, newspapers, or other materials that is spread or left on soil

natural resource—any substance found in nature that people use, such as soil, air, trees, coal, and oil

organic—material produced by animals or plants

organic produce—fruits and vegetables grown without the use of chemical fertilizers

pesticides—chemicals used to kill insects and other small creatures that harm plants

▸ Sand is mixed with gravel and cement to make concrete for sidewalks and driveways. Silica sand, which is pure quartz, is used to make glass.

▸ A kind of clay called nonexpendable clay is used for making bricks, pottery, tile, fine china, and other ceramics. Nonexpendable clay becomes soft when water is added to it and can be molded into any shape. The shaped clay is then baked in a kiln, an oven so hot that it takes all the water out of the clay. The clay permanently hardens into its new shape.

▸ A white clay called kaolin is used to make porcelain and fine china.

▸ Some soils are called mineral soils and others are called organic soils. More than 20 percent of the particles in organic soils are organic.

▸ Most gardeners do not wait for topsoil to form in their yards. They buy bags of topsoil at their local garden center. This topsoil is rich in humus. They then spread the topsoil over the old soil and plant grass or flowers.

▸ Soil temperature is important for growing plants. When the soil is too cold, plant growth stops. Most plants do not start growing in spring until the soil temperature reaches 55 degrees Fahrenheit (13 degrees Celsius). Some soils dry out and crack when they get too hot and there is no rain.

▸ With all the plants and trees that grow in a rain forest, one would think the soil is quite rich. However, just the opposite is true. Heavy rainfall washes nutrients out of the top layer of soil. Tropical plants get most of the nutrients they need through decaying plant material on the ground. Some plants get nutrients by growing on other plants.

On rare occasions, plants do not grow from soil. Here, a flowering plant grows on a tree trunk in a rain forest in Brazil.

At the Library

Farndon, John. *Life in the Soil.* San Diego: Blackbirch Press, 2004.

Graham, Ian. *Soil: A Resource Our World Depends On.* Chicago: Heinemann Library, 2004.

Gurney, Beth. *Sand and Soil.* New York: Crabtree Publishing, 2005.

Nardi, James B. *The World Beneath Our Feet: A Guide to Life in the Soil.* New York: Oxford University Press, 2003.

Stewart, Melissa. *Soil.* Chicago: Heinemann Library, 2002.

On the Web

For more information on **soil,** use FactHound to track down Web sites related to this book.

1. Go to *www.facthound.com*
2. Type in a search word related to this book or this book ID: **0756508576.**
3. Click on the *Fetch It* button.

FactHound will find the best Web sites for you.

On the Road

New Mexico Farm & Ranch Heritage Museum
4100 Dripping Springs Road
Las Cruces, NM 88011
505/522-4100
www.nmoca.org/farmandranch.html
To learn about the 3,000-year history of agriculture in New Mexico

Agricultural Heritage Museum
South Dakota State University
Box 2207C
Brookings, SD 57007-0999
605/688-6226
www.agmuseum.com
To see exhibits about the crops, livestock, and technology of South Dakota agriculture